"All over this nation, God is stirring the hearts of men to rise up and enter into their God-given destiny. Lou Turner's lifelong passion is to see men enter into their divine purpose in life. 'Living Life God's Way,' of which this book is a part, is born out of this passion. Throughout this Bible study series, Turner opens up God's Word to help you discover HIS plan for your success in your life, family, and work. If you are ready to get off the treadmill, to begin to enjoy God's fullness in your life and make a significant contribution to the world around you, I recommend that you dive into this life-transforming Bible study."

Hal H. Sacks, D.Min., *BridgeBuilders International Leadership Network*

"It seems North American culture is rapidly moving toward what the Bible calls 'everyone doing what is right in his own mind' (Judges 21:25). The prophet Isaiah declared, 'Woe to those who call evil, good, and good, evil' (Isaiah 5:20). This Bible study series will challenge every man in the 21st century as 'iron sharpens iron'! The Q&As at the end of each chapter really personalize the teaching."

Dennis Conner, *Co-Founder/President, Called to Serve Prayer-Coaching Ministry*

"I have known Lou Turner for over twenty years. Lou loves Jesus and has built his life on the Word of God. Lou's Bible study series, 'Living Life God's Way,' is full of biblical truth that has been tested and can be applied by disciples of Jesus in practical ways. These books will help you grow in your faith and gain confidence and competence, which will increase your fruitfulness in Christ.

Mark Buckley, *Founding Pastor of Living Streams Church*

Living Life God's Way

WHO YOU ARE IN CHRIST

LOU TURNER

Who You Are in Christ
Second Edition, 2023
Copyright © 2020 by Lou Turner

Who You Are in Christ is part of the Living Life God's Way Series by Lou Turner.
All rights reserved. No part of this publication may be reproduced, stored in a retrieval system, or transmitted in any form by any means—electronic, mechanical, photocopy, recording, or otherwise—except for brief quotations in critical reviews or articles, without the prior permission of the publisher, except as provided by U.S. copyright law.

Unless otherwise identified, Scripture quotations are from the ESV® Bible (The Holy Bible, English Standard Version®), copyright © 2001 by Crossway, a publishing ministry of Good News Publishers. Used by permission. All rights reserved.

Scripture quotations marked (NIV) are taken from the Holy Bible, New International Version®, NIV®. Copyright © 1973, 1978, 1984, 2011 by Biblica, Inc.™ Used by permission of Zondervan. All rights reserved worldwide. www.zondervan.com. The "NIV" and "New International Version" are trademarks registered in the United States Patent and Trademark Office by Biblica, Inc.

Some of the anecdotal illustrations in this book are true to life and are included with the permission of the persons involved. All other illustrations are composites of real situations, and any resemblance to people living or dead is coincidental.

To order additional books:
www.amazon.com
www.hislifeinus.com

ISBN: 978-1-7331186-0-6

Editorial and Book Packaging: Inspira Literary Solutions, Gig Harbor, WA
Book Design: PerfecType, Nashville, TN
Cover Design: MTWdesign, Dickson, TN
Printed in the USA by Ingram Spark

He will be like a tree firmly planted by streams of water,
Which yields its fruit in its season
And its leaf does not wither;
And in whatever he does, he prospers.

Psalm 1:3

TABLE OF CONTENTS

Preface   ix

How to Use This Book   xi

Introduction   xiii

1. Rescued for a New Life   1

2. The Christian's Present   19

3. Discovering God's Love and Grace   43

4. The Battle against Sin   55

5. Faith without Works Is Dead   69

A Final Word   77

About the Author   79

PREFACE

We live in a world that has largely forgotten what manhood is about. In the Western world, men are often portrayed on television as buffoons who are out of touch and must rely on their wives to straighten them out. These characters are portrayed as silly, insensitive, lacking common sense, and when they do speak, they are generally wrong. They are usually portrayed as either ridiculously weak or overly macho. They are not able to commit to a long-term relationship and are often guilty of mistreating women. Positive role models are hard to find in the media.

However, the Bible teaches a different type of manhood, the authentic one. Men are to be leaders, loving their wives and children, excelling in their work, and standing for truth. They are to be men of wisdom, knowledge, and godly character, seeking after God and His direction. They are to be exhibiting godly leadership at church, in the community, and in business, and to be a light to those around them. They are to be men of compassion and love, as well as courageous and bold when needed.

Men go astray from these ideals, including Christian men, due to improper convictions or beliefs about life. They have received these from various sources: well-meaning family and friends, the media, and the culture around them—a world system that promotes the tearing down of God's biblical truths.

PREFACE

But without proper biblical foundation, we will all go astray. That's why I wrote these books, containing insights, observations, and biblical truths distilled over the course of my decades of life and ministry. Each section is designed to be a stand-alone section for study and consideration. I hope this series, *Living Life God's Way*, will be used to disciple men in biblical truths for life. Whether you use it for yourself, with a group, or to mentor or disciple someone else, my hope is that it will be a blessing to you and encourage you to seek God and grow in Him.

HOW TO USE THIS BOOK

What does it mean to be a "good" husband and father?
How do I live out the Christian life at work?
What does God want from me—and how
am I supposed to find that out?

These were questions that plagued me as a young man—questions, I learned, that are at the front of many men's minds at various times in their lives. For me, these questions began my quest to seek God and discover the answers I needed. My discoveries, over the years of my life, led to this series of booklets, *Living Life God's Way*. While I do not suggest that I have discovered all of the answers, my desire is to share what I have learned and hope it will be helpful for you. This series discusses 13 topics that every man must deal with, regardless of his work, calling, profession, or circumstances. It is difficult to know how to live the Christian life without understanding what God says about these areas of life. These topics are:

1. Seeking and Finding God
2. Who You Are in Christ
3. A Man's Work and Ministry
4. Understanding Authority
5. A Man and His Wife

6. A Man and His Children
7. Getting Guidance from God
8. Overcoming Strongholds
9. A Man and Money
10. Repentance, Forgiveness, and Restitution
11. Being a Leader
12. A Man and Sex
13. The Test of Pride

You can use these books to study on your own, in a small group, or with a larger group of men. Each topic or booklet is a stand-alone study, and a person can begin with any one he chooses. They are different lengths and can be adapted to various settings—home, church, or community—all topics that are pertinent to today.

Explore what the Bible says about these important and critical parts of life. The encouragement is to read these with an open heart, asking God to reveal His truth to you in each of these areas. Pray that His Spirit will show you His truth, so that you may live in it and enjoy all God has for you. I pray that you experience the blessing and presence of God in your life as you draw closer to Him and become more aware of His leading in every area of your life.

INTRODUCTION TO WHO YOU ARE IN CHRIST

Therefore, if anyone is in Christ, the new creation has come: The old has gone, the new is here! (2 Corinthians 5:17)

Once we become followers of Jesus, we become "new creations," the Scripture tells us. Our new identity in Christ will affect our thinking, our attitudes, our outlook, and our actions. Having an understanding of what that means—our identity being in Christ—is life changing. Applying that understanding to our thinking and the way we live will change every part of your life! **That's why studying this new life is of utmost importance to every believer, and well worth our attention and consideration.**

We hear good messages in church and through teachers about grace, mercy, salvation, sanctification, judgment, repentance, faith, and hope. They may seem like lofty concepts, and bringing all of these things into our day-to-day lives may seem a bit daunting. Yet, they are something we all need to heartily go after.

For this reason, I encourage you to go into this study prayerfully, asking God to reveal His truth to you and show you how it applies to you personally. I urge you to meditate on the scriptures we'll be studying—consider them deeply and carefully. Ask the

Holy Spirit to reveal their meaning to you and to graft their truth into your heart and soul.

Let's enter this study of *Who We Are In Christ* with an open heart and open mind, hungering to know Him more. Think about the scriptures and what they mean—not just understanding the words, but what they mean to you, personally. Pray over them and ask God's Spirit to bring revelation and understanding to you. Ask Him to change your life. Ask Him for the "hidden manna" (Revelation 2:17).

In this study, we will look at what Christ has done for us and our new life in Him. We will also discuss overcoming our old way of life through the power of the Holy Spirit, and living a victorious Christian life.

Chapter 1

Rescued for a New Life

Realizing who we are, or rather, who we have *become*, in Jesus Christ, is an exciting study. Understanding our new identity—with all its benefits, changes, and challenges—is of life-changing importance to us who are now adopted as sons into God's kingdom family (see Ephesians 1:3-6). Let's get into this study. It is exciting and meaningful!

A wealthy and prominent man came secretly by night to "the teacher," as many called Him. The teacher was a controversial person and the wealthy visitor didn't want others to know of his interest in His teachings. It was safer to go by night, unnoticed, to protect his reputation and standing.

But the message of the teacher drew him and he wanted to know more. He said, "Rabbi, we know you are a teacher who has come from God, for no one could perform the miraculous signs you are doing if God were not with him."

Some said this teacher was the long-awaited Messiah. Others said He was a heretic and blasphemer. The wealthy man wanted to know, "Just who is this man?" So he came by night, in secret, to find out.

Then the teacher said something that astounded him. "I tell you the truth, unless a man is born again, he cannot see the kingdom of God."

The teacher cut to the heart of the matter. The wealthy man hungered for the kingdom of God to come. After all, his nation was occupied by Roman legions. The hope of the people was that the Messiah would come, overthrow the Romans, re-establish the sovereignty of the kingdom of Israel, and bring righteous rule to the nation.

The teacher dealt with the man's heart: he had to be born again. But how was this possible to be born again, or re-born, since he was already a grown man? What did the teacher mean, "born again"?

The teacher, who actually was the long-awaited Messiah, proclaimed that God's kingdom was in a man's heart, and came about by heart change, by spiritual rebirth—a newness of life by the transformation of the heart of man.

And so it is today. It's an astounding but simple truth. By asking Christ into our life to be our Lord and Savior, we are reborn. We become a new person in Christ. Regardless of whether or not the changes in people who receive Christ are initially great or gradual, we nevertheless become a new creation or person.

By the way, when a person receives Christ into their life, there *will* be a life change. And, as we discover who we became when we accepted Him, who we can become as we live for Him, and what we can accomplish by following Him, our new life takes on a new dimension—one of great possibilities with a new future.

I gave my life to Christ in my early twenties. I had grown up in church and had a lot of "head knowledge," meaning I had heard a lot about God and even read a lot of the Bible. But as a husband, father, and businessman, I realized I needed more than just head knowledge. I needed a living relationship with God, not just knowledge about Him.

I yearned for more, for something real, and the God I had learned about in the past wasn't enough. I needed to know Him and experience Him now, in my life and my needs.

How was I to live this Christian life? What did He want of me? How was I to think about God and relate to Him? How was I to serve Him? And most of all, did He love and care for me? I had a lot of questions that needed to be answered. I began to pray and cry out to Him to reveal Himself to me. As I did, He did.

I've learned much as I have sought God over the years, but I still have the hunger for more. That's the way it should be. As seekers, we should always want and need more of God. We have a deep need to experience His presence and be led by Him. Our inner man needs Him. We have a hunger that only He can meet. It cannot be met any other way.

The Holy Spirit will always draw us to Him, and He will plant in us both a need and hunger to know Him more. When we become a Christian, the Holy Spirit comes to live in us (Ephesians 1:13-14). He becomes active in our life as we allow Him in and yield to Him. If we do not feel this drawing by God's Spirit, we are in a potentially dangerous place. It could mean we have ignored His drawing and become complacent. Or, worse, we have developed a hardened heart.

We should always want more of Him. God's Spirit will draw us to Him. He will draw us to pray and read His Word, and there will be a hunger for fellowship with Him. If you are not feeling this, then you should immediately pray and ask His Holy Spirit to put those desires in you. Then you need to respond when He calls you to spend time with Him.

But we also need to know about who we are in Him. God's Spirit wants to reveal that to us. As we seek Him, He will give ongoing revelations about who He is, what His will is for us, and who we are in Him. Knowing who we are in Christ is not just a *good* thing to know; it is *essential* for us to know. It frees us from bondages, brings us peace in our souls, and lifts us up to a plane of living and walking with Him that we so desperately need.

It's true that as we are seeking Him, the more we get of God, the more we want. It is also true that the more we get and understand the better off we are. We live life better. We get direction from Him and we experience Him more.

Please understand, we should never be fully satisfied in this life spiritually. We should always desire more. Jesus said we should hunger and thirst for righteousness (Matthew 5:6). That means we should be hungering and thirsting for more of Him in our lives. This drives us to Him and makes the Holy Spirit more alive in our lives. Jesus said, *"Blessed are those who hunger and thirst for righteousness, for they will be filled"* (Matthew 5:6).

I love to hear stories of what God has done for others. It feeds my soul and motivates me to want to see more of God's activities in my life. I have prayed, "God, I love to read and hear of what You have done and are doing in other people's lives. But I want to see You do these things in my life."

This is a godly prayer. Wanting to see God do more in our own life is the way it should be. We should not be satisfied with just hearing about His actions in others. We should hunger for Him to be more active in our own life. But, in order to understand the new life and identity we have in Christ, and how it impacts our life, we need to understand why we *need* a new life.

There are many things in life that can mislead us or try to steal from us what God wants us to have. The world's philosophies, the things we have been led to believe, or the things we may have accepted as true, but do not agree with scripture. Anything we believe that is not what God wants for us, or that is not true according to the Bible, can hold us back or cause us to be kept from God's best for us.

The Bible also says that we have an enemy, Satan, that is working to rob us of all God has for us. *"The thief (Satan) comes only to steal and kill and destroy; I am come that they may have life, and have it abundantly"* (John 10:10).

Satan, by feeding us lies, wants to rob us of all God has for us. He is a "thief" that wants to keep us from God's best for us; the abundant life He wants us to live and experience.

Genesis chapters 1 through 3 (please read these chapters), tells the story of how Satan went to work right after God created mankind, to try to rob him of all God had for him. Satan hates the idea of mankind having a personal relationship with God and discovering His love for us. He certainly doesn't want us to realize all that Christ did for us at salvation and the life God has for us.

> **God wants us to know Him and discover all He has for us.**

The Good News of Our Salvation

We need to start with the basic truths that are the foundation for our new life. We *all* start out our Christian life with different persuasions, family cultures, and life values that may not agree with Scripture. The older we are when we accept Christ, the more we have been exposed to things we may have accepted as truth, things that need to be renewed in us. This shapes our thinking and our values. We also, prior to salvation, are separated from

God—not from His desire for us to know Him, but separated from a true relationship with Him. That gap can only be bridged through accepting Christ as our Savior, that is, being saved or "born again."

What separates us from God is our sin and our wrong thinking, and the Bible says we are all guilty of both sin and wrong thinking. Sin and wrong thinking means we do things that hurt ourselves or others. It also means we are living our life separate from God, that we have not surrendered our life to Him. *"For all have sinned and fall short of the glory of God"* (Romans 3:23). It doesn't matter to what degree we have sinned; the point is that we must come to the place of realizing we need a Savior, Jesus, and ask Him into our life.

God, because He loves us, wants to redeem us from sin and wrong thinking. Since the curse of sin is death, God sent Jesus to die for us, to take the place of everyone who accepts Him as their Savior. So Jesus came to die in man's place. He lived a perfect, sinless life and sacrificed Himself on the cross to pay the penalty for mankind's sin.

The Bible says He went into Sheol (the place of the dead), preached the gospel to those captives of death, and rose victorious over sin, death, and the grave. By accepting Him as our savior, we enter into that victory He won for us.

When we receive Christ as our Savior, many changes come into our lives:

We are washed clean. When we accept Jesus as Savior, we are washed clean from our sin, our past, our mistakes, and wrongdoings. It doesn't matter how great those wrongs are, we are forgiven. No matter what we have done, Jesus' work is greater than any sin we have committed; any wrong we have done. We read in the Psalms, *"For as high as the heavens are above the earth, so great is his* *love for those who fear him; as far as the east is from the west, so far has he removed our transgressions from us"* (Psalm 103:11-12).

Since we can travel either east or west and never reach the end, there is no measurable distance that He has removed our wrongs from us; it is infinite. All the stains in our life of our past wrongdoings are permanently removed when we accept Christ as Savior.

> *"For God wanted all of Himself to be in His Son, through Him to reconcile to Himself all things, whether things on earth or things in heaven, by making peace through His blood, shed on the cross."* (Colossians 1:19-20)

> *"For God so loved the world, He gave His only begotten son, that whoever should believe in Him, will have everlasting life."* (John 3:16)

We are freed from death. The penalty of sin, death, is also removed. Jesus died so we would not have to. Granted, we will all one day die physically. But if we have placed our faith in Christ, when we die, it is a passing from this life and we will be taken into God's presence and live forever with Him—forgiven, spotless, and loved. We read, *"Then we who are alive, who are left, will be caught up together with them in the clouds to meet the Lord in the air, and so we will always be with the Lord"* (1 Thessalonians 4:17). This passage speaks of the Lord coming to take all believers to be with Him. Once we are with Him, we will forever be with Him.

We receive a new citizenship. At salvation, we become part of a new kingdom: *"For he has rescued us from the dominion of darkness and brought us into the kingdom of the Son He loves"* (Colossians 1:13). We literally transfer our citizenship and our future into a new "kingdom," that of God and His Son Jesus Christ. We are not the same person. We have a new life!

The kingdom of God is twofold. It is His kingdom in heaven, where He is, and it is His kingdom in us. All believers are part of His kingdom. When Jesus was on Earth, His disciples thought His kingdom was coming physically on Earth with Jesus ruling all of mankind. That will happen one day in His millennial reign on Earth (see Revelation 20:4-6). But Jesus told them that until then, His kingdom was one inside people on Earth. His truth, His promises, and His power on Earth were to be manifested through them, and now us as His followers. That's why His Spirit is given to us when we become believers in Him. *"Blessed be the God and Father of our Lord Jesus Christ, who has blessed us in Christ with every spiritual blessing in the heavenly places, even as He chose us in Him before the foundation of the world, that we should be holy and blameless before him. In love He predestined us for adoption to Himself as sons through Jesus Christ, according to the purpose of His will, to the praise of His glorious grace, with which He has blessed us in the Beloved. In Him we have redemption through His blood, the forgiveness of our trespasses, according to the riches of His grace, which He lavished upon us, in all wisdom and insight making known to us the mystery of His will, according to His purpose, which He set forth in Chris as a plan for the fullness of time,to unite all things in Him, things in heaven and things on Earth"* (Ephesians 1:3-14).

His plan was predestined before the creation of the Earth for all who accepted Him to be a part of His kingdom. His Spirit is there to give us the power to live for Him and to do His work on Earth, as we see in these passages:

"But you shall receive power when the Holy Spirit has come upon you" (Acts 1:8)

"For our gospel did not come to you in word only, but also in power and in the Holy Spirit and with full conviction" (1 Thessalonians 1:5)

"Does God give you the Spirit and make such powers active in you by your doing what the Law says or by the truth you hear and believe?" (Galatians 3:5)

"And because you are sons, God sent into our hearts the Spirit of His Son, who cries Father! So you are no longer a slave but a son. And if you are His son, God has made you His heir" (Galatians 4:6-7).

We are redeemed from our past life to a new life, we are forgiven of our past sins and wrongdoings, and He desires to make known to us His will. We have obtained an inheritance of God's goodness through Christ, which He desires for us to know and understand. All throughout life, as circumstances come up, He desires us to know His will and purpose for us and how we are to live our life. He wants to give us understanding and release His power in us to accomplish His will in our life. *"But if any of you lacks wisdom, let him ask of God, who gives to all men generously and without reproach, and it will be given to him. But let him ask in faith without any doubting, for the one who doubts is like the surf of the sea driven and tossed by the wind"* (James 1:5-6).

The Bible clearly states that God delights to give us the wisdom we need. That would include any understanding or direction we are seeking Him for. Sometimes He gives it right away. At other times He gives it as we seek Him.

We receive all God's fullness. Further, Colossians 2:9-10 says, *"For in Christ all the fullness of the Deity lives in bodily form, and in Christ you have been brought to fullness. He is the head over every power and authority."* Other translations say we are "complete" in Him.

Think about this. All of our shortcomings can now be made complete in Christ. What we lack, He makes up for and provides to us. He is perfect and God granted all authority and power to Him. He in turn makes us an heir, a partaker of all God has granted to Him. All He has is now ours. He makes up for all of our shortcomings and weaknesses. I encourage you to pray about this and ask God to help you understand what this means to you and your life. Grasping this is life changing! (And by the way, learning about this happens all through life as we seek Him, not all at once.)

We become sons and heirs of God. We have gone from being estranged or separated from God to being His sons. Galatians 3:26 says, *"For you are all sons of God through faith in Christ Jesus."* This is a total change of our lives and destiny.

Christ causes us to enter into all of His promises from the Father. Romans 8:16-17 says, *"The Spirit himself testifies with our spirit that we are God's children. Now if we are children, then we are heirs—heirs of God and co-heirs with Christ, if indeed we share in his sufferings in order that we may also share in his glory."*

God the Father has given all to Jesus; His Son and heir of all things. The amazing thing is that you and I have become joint heirs with Christ of all that is His!

Do you begin to get the (marvelous) picture? You and I are now "in Christ." All that the Father has given Him is now also ours. You are an heir of all Christ has—and that is all that God has. It is unbelievable that we, who were sinners and estranged from God, are now His children and heirs of all He has. His love is great. His plan is great. His mercies endure forever!

What about you? If you have never asked Jesus Christ to come into your life to be your Savior, this is a great time to do it. You just have to humble yourself before Him, admit you need saving, and ask Jesus to come into your life. If that describes you, let's pray together right now: *"Dear God, I realize I need Jesus to come into my life to be my Savior. I ask You, Lord Jesus, to save me from my sin. I accept You as my Lord and Savior. Amen."*

If you prayed that prayer and meant it, you are now a Christian! You have joined God's family! You have been changed from death to life, and are now a new person.

A Change So Great It Required a New Name

The concept of being changed, or becoming a new person, comes up repeatedly in the Bible. You'll see it over and over again.

In Genesis 17, God did a unique thing in the life of a man named Abram. (In fact, take a few minutes right now and read that passage in your own Bible.) God began to reveal His plan for Abram's life. He was going to make Abram the father of many nations. And then God changed Abram's name, from Abram to Abraham.

The name "Abraham" was appropriate since it meant "father of a multitude." However, the name change is even more significant than that. God had just given Abraham the covenant of circumcision, a rite that was to be practiced by all of Abraham's descendants. Circumcision is the removal of the foreskin from the male reproductive organ.

You may be wondering why I would bring this up. Is this relevant for us? Yes, it certainly is—because circumcision was symbolic of the new covenant of salvation through Christ. In Christ, our old man (or old sinful self), is removed by the work of Christ through the Holy Spirit. Our nature is changed and the old self is made new through the work of Jesus on the cross. It is sealed by the indwelling of the Holy Spirit, God's seal of His new covenant with us (Ephesians 1:13-14).

God gives us His Holy Spirit to help live out the new life He has put in us. In other words, in salvation, our old life dies and a new one begins. From this point forward the "old man" has been crucified (Romans 6:6) and we now start to learn to yield our lives to the Holy Spirit to live out our new life.

Circumcision was a symbolic representation of the old man, or the flesh, being removed and the new man, or new covenant, being realized through salvation. Jesus Himself said, when asked how we can be part of God's kingdom, *"You must be born again"* (John 3:3,7). So Abram, because of this covenant of circumcision he had with God, became Abraham. His new name was to represent his new life of covenant with God.

> **Abraham's new life brought on a new identity.**
> **His new name was to show he was a new person**
> **because of God's covenant or promises to him.**

Similarly, in the New Testament, we learn how the Apostle Paul's name was changed from Saul to Paul. As Saul was traveling to Damascus, Jesus supernaturally revealed Himself to Saul. The experience on that road changed Saul's life. (Again, take a few minutes to read Acts 9 in your Bible.). Saul went from persecuting Christians to becoming one himself. God changed Saul so drastically that He gave Him a new name because he was a new person; a radically changed one.

This name change would have been especially meaningful to Paul as he was a scholar of the Scriptures. Knowing of Abraham's name change, he would recognize that his own name change represented his new life. Similarly, the Apostle Peter's name was actually Simon, but Jesus changed it to Peter. Abraham's grandson Jacob's name was changed to Israel. These name changes reflected the new identity God had for these men and His plan and destiny for them.

In the same way, when you and I become Christ-followers, our life changes. In the book of Revelation, when Jesus was addressing the church in Pergamos, He said that those who are overcomers will receive a new name in Heaven, written on a white stone, which only they will know (Revelation 2:17).

We don't know what that name is. Possibly the meaning of the new name will identify our character or our heart towards God. Or it may identify our eternal purpose or calling. But the interesting thing is that each of the overcoming saints will receive a new name. When God sees us, He sees not only who we are, but His plan for us and who we can become.

New Life in Christ

Because of the work of Christ, when we accept Him as Savior:

- We are forgiven all our sins. We are washed clean.
- We are born again and become children of God. Our relationship with God is established.
- Our fellowship with God is also established
- We become a joint heir of all Christ has been given by God the Father.
- The power of the curse of sin and death is broken in our lives. Our old man dies.
- The Spirit of God comes to dwell in us to empower us to live the new life God desires us to have.

Sin brought death. Jesus brought life. When we believe on Him, we accept His death as a substitute for our required death due to sin. As a result of Christ's death, we receive eternal life. John 3:16 says, *"For God so loved the world that he gave his one and only Son, that whoever believes in him shall not perish but have eternal life."*

That is the good news of the Bible: Jesus coming to Earth. His life, death, and resurrection comprised the single most important event in all of mankind's history. He redeemed us from sin and restored our lost fellowship with God. Praise God! He has rescued us from sin, the curse of sin, and death. We are redeemed in this life to restored fellowship with Him, and redeemed for eternity to live with Him in Heaven.

Even better yet, Jesus took the keys of death, hell, and the grave and gave them to the Church (Matthew 16:18-19). The reason Satan had the keys to death, hell, and the grave was because of the sin of Adam that all men shared. Since mankind is sinful, he cannot enter heaven and be with God—he is sin-stained. The sin of Adam and our own sins must be taken away and we must be washed clean of our sin. Since mankind was sinful, in death he was cursed to be away from God. Since Satan had dominion over death, mankind was under the curse of death away from God where Satan had dominion.

The parable of Lazarus in Luke 16 says that even the righteous dead were separated from God until Christ came. Lazarus, in this passage, was in Abraham's bosom and separate from the rich man, who was in torment. There was a gulf between them. Nevertheless, both were separated from the presence of God. When Christ arose, the righteous dead went with Him to heaven, and the keys to death, hell, and the grave were taken from Satan. Those who accept Christ go to be in the presence of the Lord forever when they die. No longer does death hold any power over us. We are free from that (see 1 Thessalonians 4:17)!

The Crown of Thorns

In Genesis chapter 3, when Adam disobeyed God, sinned, and broke fellowship with Him, God pronounced a curse upon the work of mankind through Adam.

> *"Cursed is the ground because of you: through painful toil you will eat of it all the days of your life. It will produce thorns and thistles for you, and you will eat the plants of the field. By the sweat of your brow you will eat your food until you return to the ground, since from it you were taken; for dust you are and to dust you will return."* (Genesis 3:17-19)

Because of Adam's sin and disobedience, God placed a curse on him and his work. God said "thorns and thistles" would be a by-product of his efforts. Yes, labor would produce good, but also bad.

However, Jesus wore a crown of thorns on the cross. This symbolized that the curse of thorns and thistles was broken. In fact, all curses were broken by Jesus' work on the cross. Part of being a new creation is that all curses are broken in our life. By faith, we can walk away from the old consequences of sin, heritage, and past mistakes. The curses of the past are broken and we now have a new life in Christ.

It doesn't matter who we were, how we were raised, what mistakes we made, or what our heritage was. The new life God has for us changes all of that. If our past was bad, it can no longer hang onto us. By faith, as we renew our minds and allow God to change our hearts, our new person and our new life comes forth.

Satan tells us we are doomed by our past. Jesus tells us we have a new life in Him: *"The thief comes only to steal and kill and destroy; I have come that they may have life, and have it to the full"* (John 10:10).

God has a new life for you and you may not have realized all He has for you. Seek Him for your new life and God's path for you.

QUESTIONS FOR REFLECTION AND DISCUSSION

1. Have you struggled with believing your sins have been forever forgiven? If so, why?

   _____
   _____
   _____
   _____

2. Do you see God as a loving, forgiving God? If not, why do you think you cannot?

   _____
   _____
   _____
   _____

3. Review the list of what you have received when you accepted Christ as Savior. Which of those facets would you like to know more about or begin to experience more tangibly?

   _____
   _____
   _____
   _____

TAKE A KNEE

Let's bow before the Lord in prayer. If you are unable to bow on your knee, then bow before the Lord in your heart. Let's pray: *"Father, thank You for loving me, and for what You have done to redeem me from my sin and my old life. Thank You that You desire to have a personal relationship with me. Open my eyes to understand these truths in a greater way and how they apply to my life. I want to live my new life in You. In Jesus' name, amen."*

Chapter 2

The Christian's Present

Becoming a Christian means more than just being forgiven. We are completely made new, and we become a "new" person. The Bible states that we are now able to live a different life, a new life. In fact, we are commanded to live this life.

The Apostle Paul wrote, *"So I tell you this, and insist on it in the Lord, that you must no longer live as the Gentiles do, in the futility of their thinking"* (Ephesians 4:17). He was saying they were now "in Christ" and should live this new life based upon their new status. They should no longer live as the non-Christians (Gentiles) do. He knew there would be a change because we have come to Christ. We now need to follow Christ. This new life affects our identity (who we have become) and daily lives (how we would now live).

The above scripture states we can no longer live in the futility of our wrong thinking. The simple truth is we cannot become who God's wants us to be without having our thinking changed. We must experience "mind renewal."

> *"Do not conform any longer to the pattern of this world, but be transformed by the renewing of your mind. Then you will be able to test and approve what God's will is— His good, pleasing and perfect will."* (Romans 12:2)

Scripture is clear. We cannot know God's will for our lives, and be transformed by knowing His truth for our life, without having our minds renewed. We can only know His will and His truth by knowing and studying His Word, the Bible. God's great favor toward us is revealed in His Word. The truths we need to live by are in His Word. Being transformed into the person He wants us to be is by *knowing and living* the truths of His Word.

The world throws at us constantly what it wants us to believe. Satan constantly accuses us in our minds, reminding us of our past mistakes, our shortcomings, our weaknesses, and how unqualified we are to serve God. Guess what? We are unqualified. But through Christ, we become qualified!

We need to believe the truth and stand on that to be transformed into the person God wants us to be.

Do you want to be transformed? Want to become the person God wants you to be? Want to walk with God through life?

You can.

Be transformed.

God will transform you as you ask Him to!

The Changed Life

The Apostle Paul described the difference between the life of people who don't know God and those who do:

> *They [those without God] are darkened in their understanding and separated from the life of God because of the ignorance that is in them due to the hardening of their hearts. Having lost all sensitivity, they have given themselves over to sensuality so as to indulge in every kind of impurity, and they are full of greed.*
>
> *That, however, is not the way of life you learned when you heard about Christ and were taught in him in accordance with the truth that is in Jesus. You were taught, with regard to your former way of life, to put off your old self, which is being corrupted by its deceitful desires; to be made new in the attitude of your minds; and to put on the new self, created to be like God in true righteousness and holiness. (Ephesians 4:18-24)*

God's Word says we are no longer to walk (live) the way we did prior to salvation. Rather, we are to live according to the new life God has for us. We are to "put off" the old man, and be "made new" in our thinking. We have a "new self" inside us, created by the regeneration of our spirit when we accepted Christ, and empowered by the indwelling of God's Spirit.

This point is emphasized in Colossians 2, where the Apostle Paul uses the picture of circumcision to describe the change from the old life to the new:

> *In him also you were circumcised with a circumcision made without hands, by putting off the body of the flesh, by the circumcision of Christ, having been buried with Him in baptism, in which you were also raised with Him through faith in the powerful working of God, who raised Him form the dead. And you, who were dead in your trespasses and the uncircumcision of your flesh, God made alive together with Him, having forgiven us all our trespasses, by canceling the*

record of debt that stood against us with its legal demands. This He set aside, nailing it to the cross. He disarmed the rulers and authorities and put them to open shame, by triumphing over them in Him (Colossians 2:11-15, ESV).

This passage emphasizes the fact that His work "put off" our "old self" that is ruled by the flesh. This happened by the *"circumcision of Christ, having been buried with him in baptism."* Jesus stated in Luke 12:50, *"But I have a baptism to be baptized with and how distressed I am till it is accomplished!"*

The baptism He is speaking of here are the events of His death, burial, and resurrection. When we experience water baptism, where we are immersed in water, we are symbolically entering into what Jesus is talking about. We are "buried" with Him and are raised with Him into new life. Baptism is a picture entering into His death, burial, and resurrection, therefore being able to triumph over sin in our life.

Ultimately, Jesus triumphed over all "powers and authorities." This means He disarmed Satan's ability to rule over us through the power of sin. Furthermore, Jesus established Himself as rightful ruler over all the earth, by taking back what Satan had gained when man sinned; the keys to death, hell, and the grave (Colossians 2:910). Through accepting Him by faith, we have been grafted into that work. We have entered into His death, burial, resurrection, and the resulting victory. We are joint heirs with Him!

Now we are to live in the light, or God's truth:

For you were once darkness, but now you are light in the Lord. Live as children of light (for the fruit of the light consists in all goodness, righteousness and truth) and find out what pleases the Lord. Have nothing to do with the fruitless deeds of darkness, but rather expose them. (Ephesians 5:8-11)

We are no longer to live the old life. In fact, we should not participate in anything that is not right for us according to God's Word. Rather, we can be a light to others to point them to God by our manner of life.

If this new life made available to us doesn't excite you, you're not getting it. You are not just saved for eternity; you have the authority of Christ available in you to triumph over sin and Satan in this life! God wants us to live the new life He has for us.

Have a problem with depression? Stop being depressed by realizing you have conquered depression through Christ. Start quoting the scriptures that say you are free. Let your mind be renewed and begin to live out the truth. Throw off depression!

Have a problem with pornography? You are set free in Christ. Begin to pray for God to change your heart and renew your mind. Quote the scriptures stating you are free and begin to throw off pornography!

Have a problem with fear and doing nothing because you fear you will always fail? God wants to bless your work and your life. Memorize Psalm 1 and other scriptures that talk of God's blessings on your life. Have confidence He is with you and will help you in all you do! Yes, challenges will come. But God will see you through all of them.

Whatever your challenge is, God wants to be in the middle of it and show He is faithful to His promises. As we trust Him and obey His Word, He will show Himself faithful in our life.

Who You Are Now

Who are we now in this new life? The Bible tells us we are:

The salt of the earth. Our lives and our presence are to "season" the earth around us. *"You are the salt of the earth."* (Matthew 5:13)

The light of the world. Light exposes darkness and brings truth. Our new life is to bring light to others—God's truth. *"You are the light of the world. A city on a hill cannot be hidden . . . In the same way, let your light shine before men, that they may see your good deeds and praise your Father in heaven"* (Matthew 5:14,16). I love the saying, "Preach at all times, and if necessary, use words." Our life is to be a light to others.

A child of God. (John 1:12). We are not separated from God; we are His children.

Part of the true vine. We are a part of Christ, the true vine, bearing good fruit in the world. *"I am the vine and you are the branches. If a man remains in Me and I in him, he will bear much fruit; apart from Me you can do nothing."* (John 15:1-5) God wants us to bear fruit in our life. Because we are planted in Him, the way we live our life should bear the fruits of His life in us. As we do the works God calls us to, we bear fruit.

Christ's friend. Most of us have a problem with this. Being a friend of the creator God, who is also our Savior, is sometimes hard to grasp. But, amazingly, Scripture tells us it is true. *"I no longer call you servants, because a servant does not know his master's business. Instead, I have called you friends, for everything that I learned from my Father I have made known to you."* (John 15:15) God desires a deep, intimate, relationship with you. And, you can have that with Him by seeking Him through prayer, Bible study, and obeying His Spirit as He prompts you and leads you.

A slave of righteousness. By our choice, we submit to the Lord and choose to become His servants, doing His work. *"You *have been set free from sin and have become slaves to righteousness."* (Romans 6:18)

A Son of God, and a joint heir of Christ of all that is His (Romans 8:14-15; Galatians 3:26; 4:6; 8:17) The Bible says Christ was given all authority by God the Father. We share in that authority because we are a joint heir of Christ. All that is His is ours.

A conqueror over sin in this life. *"No, in all these things we are more than conquerors through Him who loved us."* (Romans 8:37) We are God's warriors. He wants to defeat the works of Satan through us as we obey Him. He wants us to be channels He can work through.

A temple, a dwelling place of God. *"Don't you know that you yourselves are God's temple and that God's Spirit lives in you?"* (1 Corinthians 3:16) When we accepted Christ, His Holy Spirit came to live in us to empower us to live for Him.

A member of Christ's body. *"Now you are the body of Christ, and each one of you is a part of it."* (1 Corinthians 12:27)

Reconciled to God. We are His ministers and His priests. *"All this is from God, who reconciled us to Himself through Christ and gave us the ministry of reconciliation: that God was reconciling the world to Himself in Christ, not counting men's sins against them."* (Corinthians 5:18-19)

Made righteous, in right standing with God. The past is washed away. We are clean before Him. *"God made Him who had* *no sin to be sin for us, so that in Him we might become the righteousness of God."* (2 Corinthians 5:21)

Righteous and holy. Because we are part of Christ, His holiness and righteousness are imparted to us. When God sees us, He sees us through Christ, as a part of Christ. Though we are imperfect, Christ's work makes us complete before God. Our status before Him is: forgiven, clean, made new, empowered to live a new life, called to a new purpose, in fellowship with God (in spite of us, because of Him), loved by Him, favored by Him, protected by Him, and destined to reign with Him.

Chosen of God and dearly loved. *"Therefore, as God's chosen people, holy and dearly loved."* (Colossians 3:12) I had a problem with this one. In my head I knew I was loved by God. But whenever things were not going well, I felt like God was mad or displeased with me. My wife, Joan, wrote down scriptures about God's love for me. I carried those around and meditated on them for several weeks. The knowing of God's love went from my head to my heart. Whenever I doubt His love because of circumstances, I read those scriptures again. He loves us and we are His beloved.

A member of a chosen race of people, a royal priesthood and a holy nation for God's own possession. We are chosen by God, called by Him to be His minister to others, and part of His holy nation. *"But you are a chosen people, a royal priesthood, a holy nations, a people belonging to God, that you may declare the praises of Him Who called you out of darkness into His wonderful light. Once you were not a people, but now you are the people of God; once you had not received mercy, but now you have received mercy."* (1 Peter 2: 9-12)

I encourage and challenge you to meditate (think on) the above scriptures. Doing this can be truly life changing. Come to know who you are and what Christ did for you. Let these scriptures get into your heart and mind and change the way you think and act!

Seeing a list like this brings up a very real issue: Who we *are* (or feel like we are, anyway) and who we are *supposed* to be often seem like two different people. These truths about how we are supposed to live and the reality of how we actually live may also be out of sync.

What then is this "new life" we have in Christ, and what does it mean practically? If we have triumphed over sin and entered into Christ's authority over Satan and the sinful life, why aren't we all living that way? If the "old man" is dead and there is a "new man" in me, why am I not able to live a sinless life?

Those are really great questions!

Positional Versus Practical

The Apostle Paul wrote, *"For we know that our old self was crucified with Him [Christ] so that the body ruled by sin might be done away with, that we should no longer be slaves to sin—because anyone who has died has been set free from sin"* (Romans 6:6-7). **This defining statement means that we have been freed from sin and the old life.**

Then what's wrong here? Why are we not experiencing this? What's wrong with this picture? The truth is this: When we accepted Christ, we obtained our inheritance through Him. We now have the position of being in Him, and all He has is ours. However, practically, we may not be experiencing what we have obtained positionally. That's why understanding the change God has brought is of paramount importance to your walk with God.

> *Positionally, through Christ we*
> *have been granted victory*
> *over all sin and the flesh.*
> *But we may not be experiencing*
> *it, or living it, practically.*

When we become Christians, God's Holy Spirit comes to live in us (Ephesians 1:13,14). His Spirit now gives us the power to live the life God wants us to live. We receive the Holy Spirit into our life at salvation. However, in the book of Acts, there was a second experience with the Holy Spirit. People received a "baptism" or "filling" of the Holy Spirit. The apostles and early church leaders put great importance on this experience, as we all should.

In Acts 8:14-17, the church leaders heard that people in Samaria had received the gospel and had become believers. They sent Peter and John to pray for them to receive the baptism of the Holy Spirit. These people had already believed and accepted the gospel. They had already become Christians, and so according to Ephesians 1:11-14, they had received the Holy Spirit in their spirits as Christians. But the early church wanted them to receive more: they wanted them to receive the "filling" or "baptism" of the Holy Spirt so that they would have the power of the Holy Spirit working in their lives as the apostles did. So they laid their hands on them and prayed for them to receive the Holy Spirit baptism that they themselves had, and they received the baptism or filling of the Holy Spirit. Also the apostle Paul, in Acts 19:1-7, laid his hands on new believers and prayed they would receive the Holy Spirt baptism, which they did. Obviously, Paul realized the Holy Spirit was given at salvation to all. But he prayed for a "filling" of the Spirit for these new believers beyond salvation. He wanted them to walk in the power of the Holy Spirit.

The early church felt the filling or baptism of the Spirit was very important to all believers. They wanted all believers to receive this. So now, we all should ask for the Holy Spirt to fill us or baptize us with His presence and learn to walk in the power of the Spirit. He is there to guide us and empower us to do all that God leads us to do. God leads us by the Holy Spirit, speaks to us through the Spirit, and empowers us by His Holy Spirit. He also gives the church gifts of the Spirit spoken of in Romans 12:1-8, I Corinthians 12, and Ephesians 4:11-16. Certainly today we need the power of the Holy Spirit in our lives and the gifts He desires to give us to serve Him. We should ask God to fill or baptize us with His Spirit and manifest the gifts He has for us in our life.

Paul stated that we have a responsibility to receive all God has for us and to learn to walk in His will and purpose for us. He explained in the book of Romans:

> *In the same way, count yourselves dead to sin but alive to God in Christ Jesus.* ***Therefore do not let sin reign in your mortal body so that you obey its evil desires. Do not offer any part of yourself to sin as an instrument of wickedness, but rather offer yourselves to God as those who have been brought from death to life;*** *and offer every part of yourself to him as an instrument of righteousness. For sin shall no longer be your master, because you are not under the law, but under grace (Romans 6:11-14, emphasis added).*

Paul stated that we need to seek God and offer our lives to Him. As we surrender to Him, we subsequently walk away from our old lives and into our new ones. Some things in our lives change as soon when we are saved. Because of the influence of the Holy Spirit now indwelling us, we begin to think differently, and therefore live differently. You see, since God's Spirit comes into our lives at salvation, we cannot help but change. Other things in our lives change over time as we read God's Word and realize we need to think and act differently, and we begin to do so.

But in still other areas, the change comes as we fight the good fight of faith. We fight the fight as we believe God and seek Him to make real in our life what He says is ours. We have to claim what is ours, go after it in prayer, and cooperate with God's Spirit working in us. We have a part in conquering sin in our lives, or in obtaining what God says is ours. Yes, we are forgiven and stand clean before Him because of Christ's work. Yes, we have been given the Holy Spirit to empower us. But we must begin to practice living the new life. God does not take us over and make us live His way. Rather, at salvation, He gives us the *ability* to live the new life. **We must choose to do so.** Often, we must change our thinking so that we can begin to change our living! We need to know how to think so we will know how to act. We need to ask God to change our hearts and renew our minds to think and act as He desires so we can live out the new life we have in Christ. The Bible states we are transformed by our minds, or our thinking, being renewed (Romans 12:2, 2 Corinthians 4:16, Ephesians 4:23, Colossians 3:10).

Choose Freedom

We can actually choose to live the life God has won for us. I was talking one day with Tim (not his real name). His life looked good from the outside. At church, he was always well groomed. He was successful in business, had a nice family and talked like a Christian who had it all together. However, his life was being decimated by pornography. He knew it was wrong.

When he finally confided in me, he confessed that—though he knew it was wrong—he just could not conquer it. He was addicted and was trapped. He had prayed and asked God's forgiveness and asked God to help him, but was unable to conquer this area of sin. This had been going on for some time and he felt defeated.

I asked Tim some questions. First, "Do you want to be free?" Tim answered, "Yes."

Then I told him, "You are bound because of one of two reasons. One, you don't realize you have already been granted the victory over this and you need to learn to walk in the victory you have in Christ, or two, in your heart, you are enjoying this sin and don't really want to be free. Which is it?"

Tim was stunned, as I suspected he would be, because these were strong words.

"I do want to be free," he said.

"Then," I said, "be free. If you feel bound in this area, it is only because you have given yourself over to sin and have opened the door to be oppressed by satanic forces. They are constantly tempting you and you are giving in to them. You have developed a habit in your life of giving into this sin and have opened the door to Satanic influence. You are oppressed in this area and now you must claim your freedom. You must first realize you have been given victory over both demonic forces and the flesh, which is now ruling in this area, and then begin to walk in that victory."

"He delivered us from the power of darkness and transferred us to the kingdom of the Son he loves" (Colossians 1:13).

Satan does not want us to know that he has been conquered in our lives by the work of Christ. Through Him, we have conquered all sin, including pornography. We can walk in freedom and not be bound to any sin, including pornography. We need to pray for God to give us understanding of this and then live it. We don't need to be bound to any sin. We can conquer it.

I could be that strong with Tim because God had taken me there personally. Years before, I had woken up one night at 2:00 a.m. feeling impressed that I needed to pray. I got out of bed and began to pour out my heart to God. As I prayed, my thoughts began to focus on some areas I was struggling with in my life. Some of these areas I had been struggling with for years and did not seem to be gaining any ground.

This was not an attack of the enemy where I was being accused, and where hopelessness and despair were coming on me. Rather, it was the Spirit of God showing me these areas. I was frustrated as I realized that I was not winning this battle. I began to cry out to God. I told Him I knew the Scriptures said I was to walk in newness of life, but was struggling to do so.

"Where is the victory promised to me in Christ?" I asked. "Why am I not experiencing victory over sin in these areas?"

As I prayed and cried out to God, His Spirit began to show me that, in these areas, I needed a change of heart. I also needed to battle these areas through prayer. If I wanted victory, I could have it. But first my heart needed to line up with His. I needed to ask Him to change my heart so that my desires agreed with His desires for my life. When my desires changed, then my life would change. As long as I thought it was acceptable, or even normal, to have these struggles in my life, I would not get victory over them. I needed my heart changed and my mind renewed in these areas.

I began that night to confess that my heart needed to change. I asked God to change my heart and desires to agree with His Word and His desires for me. I purposed to pray over these areas daily until I began to see victory. It didn't take long. The changes began to take place. I was experiencing the truth that Paul wrote about:

THE CHRISTIAN'S PRESENT

**Our old man was crucified with Christ!
We are no longer slaves to sin!**

QUESTIONS FOR REFLECTION AND DISCUSSION

1. Following are a series of questions about your own identity in Christ. At times we need to ask ourselves probing questions such as these, and have the courage to be honest in our answers. These questions are worth prayerfully considering. I would suggest you deal with one or two at a time and ask God to reveal any truth He desires to show you about that area. If you spent several days on these questions alone, it could be life changing.

   Sometimes we get in a hurry to complete something when what we really need is to sit before God and ask honest questions and ask for His input. If you've never done this, this is a good time to start. These questions are direct, but they are not meant to be condemning. Ask the Holy Spirit to reveal His truth to you. He does not condemn. He may convict, but never condemns. When He shows us truth about ourselves, it is so He can work in our lives to transform us. Realize you are coming to a loving God; He loves you and wants only your best. This can be a real life-changing adventure that can lead to some really good things. This would be a good time to take notes and write these down for your own benefit.

Reflection Questions: Living the New Life in Christ

I am the salt of the earth and the light of the world.

Am I active about advancing God's Kingdom?

___

Do I extend compassion to the poor, outcasts, or unlovely?

___

Am I living my life so that I am an example to others?

___

I am a member of Christ's body, part of the true vine.

Do I give generously?

___

Do I look for ways to serve others to meet their needs?

___

Do I sense the life of Christ in my inner being? Am I letting it flow through me?

___

Am I producing fruit? (John 15:1-9)

___

I am a son of God and a friend of Christ.

Do I feel like God's friend? Someone who seeks Him out and wants His fellowship?

___

Do I have an awareness as I go through my day that I am His child?

___

Do I seek His presence daily through prayer—talking *and* listening?

___

Do I feed daily in His word? Am I growing, making progress, in my relationship with Him?

___

I am reconciled to God and in right standing with Him.

Am I quick to forgive and to seek forgiveness when necessary?

___

Am I quick to receive God's forgiveness?

___

I am chosen of God and dearly loved.

Do I feel loved by God?

___

___

___

___

Am I able to allow Him to love others through me in an appropriate manner?

Do I have patience with others and can I accept them in spite of their weaknesses?

I am a member of a chosen race of people, a royal priesthood, and a holy nation for God's own possession

Am I showing leadership at home?

Do I represent the Lord's character to my family as His priest in my home?

Do I love my wife and (if married) treating her with gentleness and honor?

_____

_____

_____

_____

Am I leading my children and household in the ways of the Lord?

_____

_____

_____

_____

_____

Do I try to be a wise and trustworthy steward of the financial resources God has given me?

_____

_____

Have I asked God to fill me or baptize me with His Spirit?

If not, why not?

2. As you worked through the above list, what impressions came to your mind? It would be good to write them down. Please be as specific as possible.

3. If God is speaking to you through this, it is because He wants you to have a new and deeper walk with Him and deeper and more meaningful relationships with others. He also wants you to walk through life with more power, purpose, and assurance. What new walk are you sensing God has for you?

TAKE A KNEE

Let's pray: *"Dear Father, I want to walk in victory. I want to be free in the areas I am struggling with. I want to walk in the freedom Your Word says I have in Christ. I purpose to pray daily over these areas and I believe and confess that I can have victory and freedom in my life. Please show me the life You have for me. Reveal Your truth to me of who I am in You. I want to live the life You have for me. I want all You have for me. I do not want to settle for less than Your best."*

Chapter 3

Discovering God's Love and Grace

After I accepted Christ and began to grow spiritually, I came to realize more about all God had done for me at salvation. I was aware of my past transgressions and my need of a Savior. I understood that I could not "earn" my salvation; it was a free gift. A loving God had accepted me just as I was, with all of my past mistakes and current problems, and had showered me with His love, forgiveness, mercy, and grace.

However, there was a part I had a great struggle with in my life *after* salvation. I was very "works" oriented and was trying to earn God's favor. Part of this orientation was due to improper teaching I had received earlier in life and at churches I attended.

I worked at having a daily quiet time and living the life God desired for me. These things were right and appropriate. The part that robbed me of understanding my relationship with God was the need I felt to do these things in order for God to be pleased with me or love me. I wanted to have God's favor, so I was constantly trying somehow to "earn" it.

In my heart, I could never do enough. I would fast and pray and feel good about my effort to seek God and please Him. But the next day, I would begin to feel the need to somehow earn His favor and love again. I often lacked peace, and constantly felt like I just couldn't live up to God's standard.

When things were going well in my life, I would feel like God was blessing me (which He was) and like His favor was upon me (which it was). However, when things would go wrong or adversity set in, I would begin to wonder why I had lost His blessing and favor. I didn't know what I had done to lose it, and would strive to discover what I had to do to regain God's favor and turn the situation around. Deep inside I would feel rejected and unloved. What had I done? Why was God displeased with me?

Another troubling issue was that I agreed with God's Word about how to live my life, but my will power simply failed me at times. I would have temporary success and feel good about myself, then experience what felt like failure in my thought life, attitudes, or actions. It compelled me to get back on the "treadmill" and give more effort to getting back into God's favor. The longer this went on, the more I felt like the battle was being lost. I wanted to please God and live a victorious life, but didn't feel like I could.

This "up and down" Christian life led me to ask many questions, the biggest one simply being, "Why?" *Why* was the Christian life this way? Was it *supposed* to be this hard to serve and please God? I began to cry out to God and seek Him for answers.

Thank God, they began to come!

The Reality of God's Grace

God began to revise my thinking with a beautiful word picture from Revelation 22:

> *And he showed me a pure river of water of life, clear as crystal, proceeding from the throne of God and of the Lamb. In the middle of its street, and on either side of the river, was the tree of life, which bore twelve fruits, each tree yielding its fruit every month. And the leaves of the tree were for the healing of the nations. And there shall be no more curse, but the throne of God and of the Lamb shall be in it, and His servants shall serve Him. (Revelation 22:1-3)*

In this passage, we see a river of water flowing from the thrones of God the Father and God the Son (Jesus). On either side of the river is the "Tree of Life."

In the Bible, water usually represents the activity of the Holy Spirit, bringing life, healing, cleansing, and purifying—which it does in this case; the river is called the "river of water of life" (verse 1). The Tree of Life represents Jesus, our Savior and life-giver. Thus, flowing from God's throne is life, healing, cleansing, purifying, forgiveness, and grace. It is a constant flow with no ending. It is there for all to enjoy and experience. And on either side of the river is the tree of life that brings health and healing to all who partake. This tree is Jesus.

That's how we need to see God: a constant source of life, love, grace, truth, and forgiveness. It flows out of His presence because it is His nature. Imagine yourself wading into the river, swimming in it, immersed in it. The life in it flows through you, bathes you, covers you, strengthens you, constantly purifies and cleanses you. You feel the strength it gives. You feel God's love and complete acceptance. You don't want to leave. You see the Tree of Life on either side. You get out and taste the fruit and experience the healing of its leaves. A sense of wholeness, wellness, and being loved sweeps over you. Why would you ever leave such a place?

You begin to walk alongside the river and find a waterfall falling from the mountain of God to the earth. Immersed in it, carried along by it, you plunge down unafraid into the water below and look up. There, in the waterfall, you see a cross and you realize all of this is yours because of what Jesus did for you on the cross. He died and gave His life so you might have His life flowing in you and through you. You have been forgiven and totally accepted. You are loved, and all Jesus has now is *your* inheritance. You hear a voice, "Welcome home, my beloved son."

As I sought God in my frustration and perceived failure, this was the picture I realized I needed to grasp and understand. In this picture, no matter where I walked I could not get away from the waterfall. It was always there. No matter where I was or what I did, His waterfall of love and grace was either next to me or behind me, for me to plunge into. It was there for the taking.

What I had been having a hard time grasping was that *grace is God's unmerited favor poured out to us.* We cannot earn it. We don't deserve it. It is just there. I am loved and accepted. You are loved and accepted. God's grace is being poured out as a waterfall to me and to all who accept Him. Yes, we have to seek the truth and live by it. The Bible teaches us to do this. But as we do, His grace and mercy are about us and poured out for us.

When we become Christians, we experience His grace toward us. All of our sins and past mistakes are washed away. In fact, the Bible says God chooses to forget them (Hebrews 8:12). It's not that He can't remember; He chooses not to. Other people may not forget our past failures or shortcomings. We may not forget them. But God chooses to forget them. His grace is poured out upon us like a waterfall, and we are cleansed and washed clean. What we also need to understand is that His grace and love is poured out not only at salvation, but continuously afterwards.

All of our past, present, and future sins, our mistakes and shortcomings, are covered by His grace.

We are continually being washed and cleansed. We are His beloved children. We cannot escape His love. *"For I am convinced that neither death, nor life, nor angels, nor principalities, nor things present, nor things to come, nor powers, nor height, nor depth, nor any other created thing, will be able to separate us from the love of God, which is in Christ Jesus our Lord"* (Romans 8:38-39).

Beware the Voice that Tries to Tell You Otherwise

Satan is rightly called the accuser of all believers (Revelation 12:10). He is constantly accusing us, making us feel unworthy and trying to rob us of our rightful relationship with God. Jesus called him a liar and the father of all liars (John 8:44).

Satan will try all kinds of ways to deceive you, constantly trying to convince you that you are unloved. He will whisper that you do not deserve God's love. If you listen to him and focus on your weaknesses and shortcomings, you will find yourself agreeing with him. That's what I was doing.

Know this: the enemy is deceiving us and robbing us! Our inheritance in Christ brings God's forgiveness, love, and grace. It is always there; we cannot escape it. The Apostle Paul wrote of this. Let's read this again in another translation. *"For I am convinced that neither death nor life, neither angels nor demons, neither the present nor the future, nor any powers, neither height nor depth, nor anything else in all creation, will be able to separate us from the love of God that is in Christ Jesus our Lord"* (Romans 8:38-39).

Understanding this changed my life. I no longer needed to try to earn God's love and favor. I couldn't; it was already there in abundance.

From then on, after I had this great revelation and realization, when the great liar and deceiver Satan began to accuse me, I realized that the enemy was trying to discourage me and get me to lose the confidence I was to have because I belonged to Christ. I often thought of the waterfall and imagined myself turning and walking into it. I realized that God's grace is being poured out upon me wherever I am. I cannot escape it.

Satan tries to get me to focus on myself, to look at my shortcomings, my failures, and my weaknesses. He wants me to focus on me and how undeserving I am.

I can confidently say that God's grace is being poured out on me because **He loves me.**

We *Are* Undeserving—Yet Righteous

The law of God in the Old Testament points out our shortcomings. Have you noticed, for example, that we cannot ever keep *all* of the Ten Commandments? Have you ever lusted or coveted what another has? Have you ever dishonored your parents? Do you ever give anything first priority before God (which is idolatry)? If so, you have broken God's law. Beyond these, there is a multitude of other laws to keep. As we see the law and all it says we must do to be righteous, at some point we will throw up our hands and say, "I can't do it! I can't live up to it all."

But as we just learned, we have received the "abundance of grace" through Jesus. We have received His *free* gift. You are made righteous! You are justified! These are a gift from Christ because of His work on the cross. John 1:17, *"For the law was given through Moses, but **grace and truth** came through Jesus Christ"* (emphasis added).

Rules and regulations do not save us; Jesus does. Moses gave us the law, which was given to reveal to us our inability to be righteous on our own. We can try to be righteous by working as hard as we can to keep the laws of God. But we will always fail.

Jesus came to give us a new life, an abundant one, full of God's grace and truth:

> *But because of his great love for us, God, who is rich in mercy, made us alive with Christ even when we were dead in transgressions—it is by grace you have been saved. And God raised us up with Christ and seated us with him in the heavenly realms in Christ Jesus. (Ephesians 2:4-6)*

Praise God; we don't have to save ourselves.

We *Are* Weak—Yet Powerful

Satan wants you to believe he still has power over you, or that because of your weaknesses you cannot live this new life. However, through God's grace and the power of the Holy Spirit, we *are* able to live the new life: *"He has delivered us from the power of darkness and translated us into the kingdom of the Son of His love"* (Colossians 1:13).

We now have the ability to live a new life. In Romans 6, the Apostle Paul writes:

> *Or don't you know that all of us who were baptized into Christ Jesus were baptized into his death? We were therefore buried with him through baptism into death in order that, just as Christ was raised from the dead through the glory of the Father, we too may live a new life. For if we have been*

> *united with him in a death like his, we will certainly also be united with him in a resurrection like his.*
>
> *For we know that our old self was crucified with him so that the body ruled by sin might be done away with, that we should no longer be slaves to sin—because anyone who has died has been set free from sin. Now if we died with Christ, we believe that we will also live with him (verses 3-8).*

Not only do you not need to strive to earn God's favor and work your way out of sin, the very *power* of sin in your life was broken by the work of Jesus on the cross:

> *For he has rescued us from the dominion of darkness and brought us into the kingdom of the Son he loves, in whom we have redemption, the forgiveness of sin.*
>
> *Once you were alienated from God and were enemies in your minds because of your evil behavior. But now he has reconciled you by Christ's physical body through death to present you holy in his sight, without blemish and free from accusation—if you continue in your faith, established and firm, and do not move from the hope held out in the gospel. This is the gospel that you heard and that has been proclaimed to every creature under heaven, and of which I, Paul, have become a servant. (Colossians 1:21-23)*

We might fail at times, or make mistakes or bad decisions. That is not the issue. Regardless of our mistakes, God's grace and the power of the Holy Spirit are always available to us. We can always run back to the waterfall of grace, love, and cleansing and be restored. The Holy Spirit, released by God's love and grace, is there to fill and empower us.

God also stands ready to give us any understanding or wisdom we need if we are trapped or need His guidance to change an area of our life. *"If any of you lacks wisdom, let him ask God, who gives generously to all without reproach, and it will be given him"* (James 1:5). Notice it says He gives it generously and without reproach. He stands ready to help us when we cry out to Him. He wants to give us wisdom and we don't have to beg Him for it.

His grace gives me the strength to stand against sin and temptation and live the life He desires for me. I can't do it in my will power alone or by my own strength. I tried that and it didn't work. If I focus on myself and my abilities, I fail. But when I focus on God's grace and love toward me, I find a new strength to overcome sin and temptation. The power of the enemy quickly fades and I have the ability to stand.

When you are tempted, try saying out loud, "I am the righteousness of Christ," again and again and see what will happen. You will see strength come to overcome the temptation as you confess this. It's pretty hard to give in to temptation when we are declaring this!

Is our faith the source of our hope and trust? Or are our trust and hope in God, the *source* of our faith? I suggest that the reason Satan attacks our hope and trust is that he knows it will undermine and destroy our faith. How can we have faith in someone we cannot trust? How can we have peace if we do not trust in God and His love toward us? Believing that God loves us, that His grace is indeed poured out on us, and that He is faithful, causes us to trust and have hope in Him. That releases our faith in Him. God's love is the source of God's grace, His unmerited favor. His love also caused the Holy Spirit to be poured out on you and me when we received Christ (Ephesians 1:13-14). We should be confident His Spirit is always with us to help us, strengthen us, teach us, and guide us.

Paul assures us that we are *"complete in Him, who is the head of all principality and power"* (Colossians 2:10). We are always "in Him." We don't deserve it, but it is true. We may have a problem accepting this, as I did, because we focus on ourselves and our "works" instead of on Him and His work. When we focus on us, we say, "No way can this grace be true." But when we focus on Him, the work He did for us, and what the Bible says He did, we must say, "Yes, it's true!"

QUESTIONS FOR REFLECTION AND DISCUSSION

1. How do you think it might change a man's approach to the Christian life if he were fully convinced he were loved and accepted? How would he be different?

2. What does the word *grace* now mean to you?

3. Have you had a hard time seeing yourself as loved by God unconditionally? If so, why? Has that changed after studying this chapter?

TAKE A KNEE

Let's pray: *"Father, please reveal Your love and grace for me. Open my eyes to understand what this means to my life. I want to walk in Your love and grace and in the power of Your Holy Spirit. I love You Lord. Thank you for all You have done for me."*

Chapter 4

The Battle Against Sin

Let's discuss the battle we all are in. We all have an enemy to overcome. We have our outward enemy, Satan and his forces, and the world system and its lies. And we have an inward enemy. The Bible calls it "the flesh." In Romans 7, Paul talks frankly about a battle against the flesh that sounds all-too-familiar to many of us: *"For I have the desire to do what is good, but I cannot carry it out. For I do not do the good I want to do, but the evil I do not want to do—this I keep on doing"* (Romans 7:18-19).

However, as we have seen, there is hope. **The good news is we have the ability to rule over the flesh and live a life of victory.** Our "new man," empowered by the Holy Spirit, is able to conquer the flesh. By seeking God and yielding to His Spirit, we can conquer sin and overcome it. These are not just words or good doctrine. This is truth. God's Word says it is so.

The Battleground

In Romans, Paul spends the majority of chapter 7 talking about the "flesh," the part of us that is attracted to sin. Even though the "old man" (that part of us that was our sinful nature) died when we accepted Christ, we still have as part of our human nature the flesh to which sin can appeal. Satan will tempt our flesh in order to get us to succumb to it. Galatians 5:19-21 describes things that tempts our flesh:

> *"The acts of the flesh are obvious: sexual immorality, impurity and debauchery; idolatry and witchcraft; hatred, discord, jealousy, fits of rage, selfish ambition, dissensions, factions and envy; drunkenness, orgies, and the like. I warn you, as I did before, that those who live like this will not inherit the kingdom of God."*

If we give into the desires of the flesh, we begin to live in the flesh or in *sin*. Even though we are a new creation and Christ has broken the power of the sinful nature, we can choose to participate in sin and it can still have a negative impact on us.

Yes, God has saved us from sin and provided for our forgiveness, but the consequences of succumbing to sin can affect us. If we have a pattern of yielding to temptation it can affect us significantly. Immorality can cost us our family or give us sexually transmitted diseases. Rebellion can cost us our job. Anger can cost us relationships and hurt others.

Continual yielding to an area of sin can cause real bondage in our life as a stronghold can be established. Our relationship with God can be affected, and we can develop a hardened heart toward God. We can be deceived by sin and begin to accept sinful things as okay in our life or in society. But the stronghold can be broken by repenting and seeking God to change our heart and renew our mind. As we seek God and meditate on His Word, the truth will set us free along with prayer and yielding to God's Spirit.

After writing in Romans 7 about the struggle against the flesh, in chapter 8 Paul states, *"Therefore, there is now no condemnation for those who are in Christ Jesus, because through Christ Jesus the law of the Spirit of Life set me free from the law of sin and death. For what the law was powerless to do in that it was weakened by the sinful nature, God did by sending His own Son . . .* (Romans 8:1-3).

So, we do not have to live giving into the flesh. *"The law of the Spirit of life has set you free in Christ Jesus from the law of sin and death"* (Romans 8:2).

We can live an overcoming life and conquer sin.

But we can't do it alone. As I discovered, willing ourselves to gut it out and live the Christian life in our own strength results in temporary victories and then failures. Obviously, our will is an asset when yielded to God. But we cannot live the Christian life and conquer the temptations of sin purely by willing it. We need to ask God to fill us with His Spirit, and ask Him to change the desires of our heart so that they agree with His desires for us. We cannot live an overcoming life without seeking God and yielding to Him. He is the one who gives us the power to overcome sin as we take simple actions with Him:

1. We yield ourselves to God by asking Him to change our hearts wherever needed so that our desires align with His. It is His Spirit who does the work. This is a key element to conquering sin in our life.

    I was driving home one night when I realized I needed a heart change. I had been fighting the good fight to live as God wanted me to as I knew how. But it dawned on me that I needed God to change my desires, my heart, to agree with

His desires and heart for me. I began that night to ask God to change my heart and renew my mind. I have prayed that for years now and have seen God do just that. My desires have changed and my thinking about many things has also changed. This in turn has changed me.

2. We do not let sinful thoughts dwell in our minds, but render our thoughts captive to Him (2 Corinthians 10:5). It is His Spirit who moves upon us and prompts us to do so. As soon as we realize we are thinking about something we should not dwell upon, we should stop thinking about it. We cannot dwell upon wrong thinking and have right results. Renewing our minds is where many victories lie. We need to begin to think differently. We need our thoughts to agree with God's Word. As we realize the truth and accept it, we can begin to pray for God to take our new understanding and change our hearts. A changed heart and a renewed mind changes the way we live, think, and act.

3. We guard our hearts so that nothing can take root there that should not. As we pray over our hearts, it is His Spirit who empowers us to stand against temptation. We do not allow anything to take root in our hearts that should not be there.

The Bible states, *"For wisdom will enter your heart, and knowledge will be pleasant to your soul"* (Proverbs 2:10). When we seek God, His wisdom will enter our heart and change our hearts desires.

"Above all else, guard your heart, for it is the wellspring of life" (Proverbs 4:23). We guard our hearts by not thinking on things we should not, and by not allowing things to take root in our heart that should not be there. The Bible here says, *"Above all else, guard your heart."* God is saying that guarding our heart is very important.

We must not allow our hearts to go astray and allow things not of God to take root there. It will not only lead us astray, but will weaken our ability to stand. In this sense, we are to be soldiers guarding that which is precious: our hearts' desires.

As we simply begin to practice these things, we begin to live in them with God's help. Walking in the power of God's Spirit requires effort. It can be done, and the Holy Spirit is there for all believers to empower them to do so. Choosing not to seek God will lead to disappointment, a sense of emptiness, and a life of at least partially living in defeat and not seeing God work in our life as we may desire.

We Yield Ourselves to God's Spirit

At salvation, the Holy Spirit enters us, regenerates us, and marks us as "God's":

> *And you also were included in Christ when you heard the message of truth, the gospel of your salvation. When you believed, you were marked in him with a seal, the promised Holy Spirit, who is a deposit guaranteeing our inheritance until the redemption of those who are God's possession—to the praise of his glory (Ephesians 1:13-14).*

However, we do not want the Holy Spirit merely to fill our spirit; we want Him to fill our entire being. After all, remember what pours out of us when He does: love, joy, peace, patience, kindness, goodness, faithfulness, gentleness, and self-control (Galatians 5:22-23)! Against these things, Paul says, "there is no law" (5:23). This is the "fruit" of God's Spirit in our lives.

God also gives us the courage and boldness we need to be His warriors. Having the fruit of the Spirit does not mean we are wimps. His peace, love, and joy, as well as the rest of the fruit of His Spirit, are mixed with the courage Jesus showed in His life and His intolerance toward those who purposely led others astray.

Paul makes an interesting statement when he says, *"Do not get drunk on wine, which leads to debauchery. Instead, be filled with the Spirit"* (Ephesians 5:18). That phrase "be filled with the Spirit" is an imperative; that is, a command. We are commanded to be filled with the Spirit—which implies it's not a passive activity. Obviously, we cannot command God's Spirit to fill us. We realize that, as Christians, His Spirit is given to us; He lives in us. However, we are to seek His presence and desire His Spirit to continually fill us by yielding to Him. As we have previously discussed, we need to ask God to fill us and "baptize" us with His Spirit. We want all He has for us.

In the Bible, the followers of Jesus had an experience where they were baptized, or filled up, with God's Spirit. This made a great difference in their lives. They received power and boldness when the Holy Spirit was poured out on them. We should all seek to be filled, or baptized, with His Spirit, and to walk in the power of His Spirit.

The second interesting thing about the phrase "be filled" is that the verb tense in the original Greek could be translated, "Keep on being filled." That is, it is a continuous activity. Did you catch that? Being filled with the Spirit is supposed to be something we continually seek and desire. No wonder Acts 13:52 tells us that *"the disciples were continually filled with joy and with the Holy Spirit."*

This is why Paul says, *"Walk in the Spirit, and you shall not fulfill the lust of the flesh"* (Galatians 5:16). God's Spirit does not take us over and make us do things. Rather, His Spirit prompts us to obey His voice; as we do so, we are empowered to accomplish His works and overcome temptation. Remember, God has granted us the victory. We must walk in it. Think of and meditate on these truths from Scripture: *"It was for freedom that Christ set us free; therefore keep standing firm and do not be subject again to a yoke of slavery"*(Galatians 5:1), and,

"But I say, walk by the Spirit, and you will not carry out the desire of the flesh" (Galatians 5:10).

I once spoke with a man who was married but had been unfaithful to his wife a number of times. When confronted with this, his response was that he just didn't have the ability to resist the temptation.

"Hogwash," I replied. "It is a decision you can make just like any other decision. If you have truly accepted Christ into your life, His Spirit is there to help you. What you are saying is that God is not truthful. You are saying God's Word is not true. His Word says you can conquer any type of sin and His Spirit is there to empower you to do so.

The real issue is, do you want to? Do you think you are the only one tempted by moral sin or lust? Every man is tempted in these areas, as Christ was. If you want to live morally pure, you can. Again the question is, do you really want to? Satan wants you to believe you do not have the ability to overcome this sin. But God says you do. Whom do you want to believe?"

The same questions apply to all of us, regardless of what areas of temptation are a particular struggle for us. When our heart is not aligned with God's, we can yield to the flesh and give ourselves over to it. Or we can yield to God's Spirit and give ourselves over to Him.

God's Holy Spirit is always present with us, to grant us power and to give us the wisdom and insight we need. Most important, there is no condemnation for us when we fail. God does not condemn us, Satan does. God's Spirit is always there to forgive, redeem, empower, and love us. Remember the waterfall of grace? We can always turn to God, walk back into the waterfall, and receive His love and forgiveness.

We Do Not Let Sinful Thoughts Dwell

We have talked about guarding our hearts and minds. As we stand against Satan's tactics and battle, his efforts to try to get us to compromise and sin, we cannot let sinful thoughts dwell in our minds, but render our thoughts captive to God (2 Corinthians 10:5). Temptation begins with thoughts. If we dwell on temptation and wrong thinking, it will begin to gain a foothold. Eventually we will live out what we have been thinking about. So taking thoughts captive means we do not allow ourselves to think on things that are wrong to think about.

James 1:13-17 says:

When tempted, no one should say, "God is tempting me." For God cannot be tempted by evil, nor does he tempt anyone; but each person is tempted when they are dragged away by their own evil desire and enticed. Then, after desire has conceived, it gives birth to sin; and sin, when it is full-grown, gives birth to death. Don't be deceived, my dear brothers and sisters. Every good and perfect gift is from above, coming down from the Father of the heavenly lights, who does not change like shifting shadows.

God does not tempt us, Satan does. The temptation begins in our thoughts. If we dwell on it, it drops from the head to the heart and can take root there. Then as we allow the desire to take root, we begin to act on it and live it out. We must stop temptation in its tracks: in our thoughts.

WE DO NOT HAVE TO THINK ABOUT *ANYTHING* WE DO NOT WANT TO THINK ABOUT.

That is why we must ask God to change our hearts so that we will not *want* to think about things we shouldn't. By bringing God into the equation, His Spirit goes to work in us, freeing us from the power of sin. This freedom was granted to us at salvation. Now we need to claim it and ask God to make it real in our lives.

We Guard Our Hearts

Finally, we need to see our heart as the soil of our life. The seeds planted there will take root and sprout. Good seeds will produce good fruit, and bad seeds will produce bad fruit. That's why it's so important to be vigilant in guarding our heart. Since this is in Scripture, it is important; I will state it again. The Scriptures tell us, "*Watch over your heart* **with all diligence***, for from it flow the springs of life*" (Proverbs 4:23).

We also need to root out what may already be there and replace the bad with the good. If we allow anger, lust, deception, or other bad seed to take root, we will battle with these areas until they are rooted out. **They are rooted out by repenting, being honest and admitting they are there, and then asking God to forgive and change us. Repentance, forgiveness, asking Him to change our heart, and accepting our restoration of fellowship with Him: that is the cycle of change.**

Many times our wrong thinking is related to our insecurities and shame. Or, to our self-interest, entitlements, and striving. The world around us is constantly throwing its philosophies, ways of life, and ways of thinking at us.

At times, our wrong thinking is due to things that happened in the past—injustices, abuses, violations, or offenses. These thoughts need to be retrained into right thoughts of significance and purpose, hope and vision, purity, forgiveness, and submission to God's authority and leading.

The self-comforting mechanisms we use to comfort ourselves in the face of pain from the past can't simply be thrown off unless we replace them with the things that should be in our hearts.

- We replace injustices with trust in God's justice and goodness.
- We replace abuses with thoughts of promises of God's healing and peace.
- We replace violations and offenses with forgiveness.

If you sense you need some replacement, I encourage you to spend some reflective time with the Lord in prayer. Like David did in the Psalms, ask the Holy Spirit to help you. *"Examine me, O Lord, and prove me: try my mind and my heart."* (Psalm 26:2).

Look past symptoms to roots. Ask the Holy Spirit to give you insight, understanding, and revelation of His will. If you find something that is hindering your life and needs replacing—not just guarding—then surrender it to God and ask Him to begin to change you and set you free. I encourage you to take this important step.

As a young man, I had a problem with anger. At times I would lash out at my family. Afterwards, I would feel badly yet confused. Hadn't they done wrong things or been negligent? Didn't I need to address these things? Hadn't they ignored my instructions? This went on for years. At times I justified my actions by reasoning that it was right.

One day, I was troubled about this and began to pray. You see, I had accepted the fact that this behavior was normal and acceptable. I realized I should not be an angry man *all* of the time, but I thought that it was okay to get angry *at times* due to the circumstances. The Bible speaks of righteous anger—anger against sin and the damage it does. I am not speaking of that. I am speaking of outbursts of anger because I was inconvenienced or because those around me did not live up to my expectations. As I prayed about this the Lord began to show me I was wrong. I was hurting my wife and children and putting a barrier between us.

My children feared my anger and it hindered my relationship of love and understanding God desired me to have. I was heartbroken when I saw this. I confessed the sin of anger and asked God to change me. When I realized I needed change and asked God to change me, it began to happen.

Changed from the Inside Out

Often, our minds or thinking must be changed, or the desires of our hearts must be changed, before our actions can change. It begins with realizing we need to change and seek God for it. He is faithful and will help us. When we seek God, His Spirit goes to work in the area in which we are seeking Him. Things will happen. It did in my life.

Walking in the Spirit means we agree with God and His truth. We call a "spade a spade" and don't make excuses for wrong behavior. When we see we are falling short in an area, we seek God for His help—daily if necessary—hourly if necessary—constantly if necessary—and He goes to work on our behalf. Established strongholds can require as to pray as we go about our day and ask God to work in our life. We will obtain freedom if we want it.

Sure, we will stumble at times. We will fall short at times. But the Lord loves us, and wants to help us learn to walk in the provision for the victorious life He has for us. He does not expect us to fight this with only our will power. He wants to transform us and teach us to yield to His Spirit and live the life He has for us.

GOD IS FAITHFUL. He will respond to our prayers. God does not give us guidance for the life we are to live, and then not help us. Jesus has provided the way for us to live a victorious life and has given us the Holy Spirit to live in us to help us. As we focus on God's truth, His love and grace for us, and the provision of Jesus on the cross for us, we can live victoriously! We can run to the waterfall of love and grace, and be cleansed and empowered to defeat Satan and the flesh. We are to be victorious warriors, defeating Satan and his forces and their work. We are being set free and we are to set others free as we have opportunity to do so.

Remember, it is difficult, if not impossible, for sin to take hold if we are concentrating on God and worshipping Him. When our focus is on Him and His truth, His Spirit is empowering us to live for Him.

QUESTIONS FOR REFLECTION AND DISCUSSION

1. In Romans 7, the Apostle Paul wrote, *"For I have the desire to do what is good, but I cannot carry it out. For I do not do the good I want to do, but the evil I do not want to do—this I keep on doing"* (verses 18-19). Can you relate to this verse? If so, in what area?

   _____

   _____

   _____

   _____

2. What are one or two ways you have experienced the Holy Spirit's power and help in your life? In what way(s) would you like to experience more of Him?

   _____

   _____

3. In this season of your life, what thoughts do you particularly need to take captive?

4. From what temptations do you particularly need to guard your heart?

TAKE A KNEE

Let's pray: *"Dear Father, I want to live a victorious Christian life and overcome the areas that at times seduce me. I know it is Your desire to help me and deliver me from the things that hinder me. I give them to You now and ask You to change my heart and my desires, and to fill me with Your Spirit. I ask You to renew my mind so I will think as You want me to. I am Your servant and surrender to Your will for my life."*

CHAPTER 5

FAITH WITHOUT WORKS IS DEAD

The man was working hard, threshing his wheat in a winepress to keep it from those who would steal it from him. His land had been taken over by a strong enemy and they would routinely take the crops of the land to support their army.

While he was working, an angel appeared to him in the form of a man and said to him, "The Lord is with you, mighty warrior." This man was trying to preserve his crops out of fear they would be stolen and now an angel was calling him a mighty warrior. The Lord had sent the angel with this message, because the Lord sees us as what His plan is for us and our potential—not as who we think we are, aware of our shortcomings.

The man didn't know what to think. How could this be? He didn't feel like a mighty warrior. Then the Lord told him to deliver his people from the enemy. The man's reply was, "My family is the least in my tribe and I am the least in my family." He was saying he did not have the resources or the standing to raise an army and deliver his people.

The Lord said, "I will be with you and you will strike down the enemy as if they were but one man."

The Lord then told him to destroy the altar of a false god in his town, and sacrifice to the Lord. The man did this under cover of night. The next morning, the town saw the torn-down altar and demanded he be killed for destroying it. Not a very good start for him delivering his people.

The Bible states that the enemy amassed its large army and prepared to come against Israel. But the Spirit of the Lord came upon the man. He blew the trumpet and called his people together to fight the enemy and they responded. So the man from the least family, who was least in that family, and was anointed by the Lord, called together an army! And the people responded. God moved on the enemy to gather together for a fight so He could destroy them.

The man, Gideon, saw the mighty army and continued to have doubts. He asked God twice to confirm He was with him, which God did. Then God told Gideon to reduce his army to 300 from 32,000 men so all would know the victory was supernatural and from God. Then God gave Gideon a plan: as he obeyed, the enemy—an army of tens of thousands of men—was routed, and Gideon defeated them.

This story is in Judges chapters 6 and 7. God called a man, Gideon, who did not think he could do it, to do a mighty deed. Gideon knew it needed to be done, but didn't think he was the one to do it. The difference was that God Himself called Gideon to the task, and brought the victory against great odds.

If internet betting would have been around at that time, all bets would have been against Gideon. The enemy was too big and too strong for him to succeed. But he did!

Acting on the Truth

In the book of James, in chapter 2 verses 14 through 25, James states clearly that "faith without works (deeds) is dead." His whole book devotes itself to the topic of acting according to our convictions; what we say we believe. We cannot just say we believe things, we have to live it!

As I have said, we are to be channels that God works through. God is looking for those who will do His works on Earth. We are to be those people.

Grasping the truths we have spoken about in this booklet gives us the confidence to begin to do the works of God. When we grasp that we are His, loved by Him, accepted by Him, and commissioned by Him, we have a much greater confidence to do His works. We become an open channel for God to work through.

Satan wants us to always be on the defensive and wants us to struggle to believe God is with us—that He loves us, will work through us, and will always be there for us. Satan wants us to constantly feel inadequate, incomplete, and unworthy to do the things God wants us to do. If we feel rejected by God, how can we be bold to do His works?

James is saying our faith should naturally produce the works God wants us to do. If we have confidence God is leading us and there to supply what is lacking and needed, then we will more boldly do the works of God.

Israel was a nation of warriors. They battled to take the ground God said was theirs. Did you ever consider the different gifts all those men had? Some were farmers and loved to work the land. Some were shepherds and wanted to raise livestock. Some were merchants and traders and were gifted to buy, sell, and make money as merchants. Some were sailors and loved the sea. Some were stone masons, some were carpenters, and some were Levites and therefore priests.

But when it came time to fight for God and follow God's leading into battle, they became warriors and went out to fight the fight and win the battles God was leading them into. They didn't tell God, "Oh, I am just a _____ (you fill it in); I am not called to be a warrior." They were all called to be warriors when they needed to be, regardless of their gifts or callings.

The same is true today. We all have different gifts and callings, but we are all called to stand up for the Lord when needed. We are all called to have courage and believe God will help us when we follow His leading.

Knowing that we are God's, and that He is always with us, gives us the faith and confidence to accomplish what God calls us to do. It will give us the boldness to move out and do what we believe we are supposed to do.

Will we have obstacles? Yes. Will we at times experience setbacks? Yes. Will we at times question what we are doing? Yes. But as we seek God and feel the assurance we are doing what He called us to do, we can keep going believing He will bring us the victory He is calling us to.

The Bible is full of stories of those God called to do things they did not feel they could do. God assured them they could because He would be with them and bring the victory. Many supernatural things happened as God moved with those as they obeyed and saw God bring the victory.

Gideon, in Judges chapters 6 and 7, was so skeptical he asked God to confirm it more than once before he obeyed. He was called to fight a great army, with that enemy having a great advantage in size and power—or so it seemed, looking only at the obvious. But when he became convinced God was leading him, he obeyed and God supernaturally won a great victory through him. (By the way, God did it, but He works through people!)

Abraham and Sarah thought surely God's will had to be done a different way than how God had said. They were too old for God to accomplish the birth of Issac, the promised child. But God did just as He said in spite of them (Genesis 16, 17, 21).

The Bible states in Hebrews 11:1, that *". . . faith is being sure of what we hope for and certain of what we do not see."* It is the ability to sense God's leading—getting confirmation, and believing it will be accomplished, even though we do not know how. By faith, we begin and believe God will finish through us. Faith produces stuff. Something seems to come from nothing. We lack what we need to accomplish what we are being led to do, and God supplies what we need as we move out. Faith obeys and trusts God.

Stories of Working Faith

There are so many true stories of God doing this and honoring those obeying Him.

I love the story of George Mueller. He started with nothing and God led him to build orphanages. He did not have the money to build anything. But he trusted God and as God led him to buy property and build buildings, the money miraculously came in. What is so amazing is that he never told anyone what he needed. He prayed and sought God—and God supplied.

Once he bought the property and built the buildings, money was needed to pay salaries, pay for utilities and building and grounds maintenance, and feed, clothe, and take care of the children. He had none of this money but believed God would supply it and He always did. This was in the 1800s.

What about today? There are countless stories of businessmen and women starting businesses in their garages or basements. They prayed and believed God and, as they worked, their businesses grew and became prosperous.

There are countless stories of men starting churches in their homes and, as they sought God and obeyed Him, the churches grew to hundreds, sometimes thousands, and sometimes tens of thousands.

What about you? What might God lead you to do? We may not all be called to deliver a nation, start a church, or start a business. But God wants to use all of us in some way. He wants us to be a light and witness to those around us.

QUESTIONS FOR REFLECTION AND DISCUSSION

1. Have you felt God leading you to do something you don't think you are qualified for? If so, what is it?

   _____

   _____

   _____

   _____

2. Do you realize that if it is really Him leading you to do something, He will confirm this and, as you seek Him, show you how to begin?

   _____

   _____

   _____

   _____

3. The enemy wants to keep us from obeying God out of fear. Can you begin taking the first step?

   _____

_____

_____

_____

TAKE A KNEE

Let's pray. "Father, lead me to do the things You desire me to do. Give me wisdom and bless my efforts. Draw me into prayer and confirm to me the steps You want me to take. I choose to trust You and to obey You."

A FINAL WORD

We have just covered a lot of ground! We will grow into these truths as we seek the Lord and grasp the truth of the scriptures contained herein. You may feel like you cannot grasp all of it now. That's ok. Read it again and again and think on the meaning of the scriptures. Ask God to make it real in your life. It will begin to take root in your heart and mind and live out in your life. But remember, Jesus said,

> *Come to me, all who are weary and heavy-laden, and I will give you rest. Take My yoke upon you and learn from Me, for I am gentle and humble in heart, and you will find rest for your souls. For My yoke is easy and My burden is light (Matthew 11:28-30).*

Jesus does not expect us to immediately grow into all of these truths and live them out perfectly. We are told to seek Him, and the Holy Spirit will work in our lives to make these truths real in us. Jesus does not place a heavy burden upon us to be perfect. He gives us rest and peace.

Many times when a lot of material is covered, it may seem like a lot to understand and put into practice. But, while we are seeking God and growing in Him, He never places on us more than we can handle. While there is always more to learn, it always

A FINAL WORD

comes down to trusting and resting in Him. He is always faithful whether we understand everything or not. He loves us.

We can run to Him. He will never turn us down.

He wants us to live the life He has for us. While we do have a battle to fight, we also have been provided the tools to win the fight. Think of yourself as one who has been adopted into a royal family, who is highly loved and valued, and has been given a great and glorious future in eternity. In this life, you have been given great tools to overcome your enemies, take the truth to those around you, and live a life with peace and joy. Though you may fall, He will pick you up. Though you may fail, He is there to forgive and restore. Remember He said,

> *"The thief comes only to steal and kill and destroy;*
> ***I came that they may have life, and***
> ***have it A BUNDANTLY"!***
> *(John 10:10, emphasis added)*

ABOUT THE AUTHOR

Lou Turner wrote *Living Life God's Way* out of his passion for men to discover God, and to get to know Him and what He has for them. This 13-book men's discipleship series is the culmination of Lou's own journey—a life of seeking God, studying His Word, memorizing Scripture and meditating on it, and practical experience with family, community, marketplace work, and Christian ministry. It also comes, by Lou's own admission, from life experiences of both successes and mistakes, as a result of both good and bad decisions.

Lou has headed ministries, written and taught workshops, classes, and seminars, and discipled dozens of men. Now, he has put into print the things he has learned to help other men along their path and journey.

Most of Lou's growing up years were spent in Detroit and its suburbs, where he was raised in a pastor's home. Following his graduation from university with a Bachelor of Science in Business Administration, Lou and his wife planted and pastored a church for three years. After that time, he felt the strong call of God to return to business.

Over the years, Lou has served in numerous senior executive positions with national and international companies in the real estate and oil and gas industries. As of this writing, Lou is still active in business with his own home building company. He has

ABOUT THE AUTHOR

been married to his wife Joan since they were 20. They have three children and 10 grandchildren, and make their home in Phoenix, Arizona.

www.ingramcontent.com/pod-product-compliance
Lightning Source LLC
Chambersburg PA
CBHW021119080526
44587CB00010B/577